MARIE CURIE

Originated in Hong Kong by Modern Age
Printed and bound in China by Midas Printing Limited

For Marshall Editions:
Publisher: Richard Green
Commissioning editor: Claudia Martin
Art direction: Ivo Marloh
Editor: Sharon Hynes
Picture manager: Veneta Bullen
Production: Anna Pauletti

Consultant: Dr Jeff Hughes
Design and editorial: Tall Tree Ltd
Cover: QED Publishing

Previous page: Marie Curie in her laboratory.
Opposite: Marie and her husband, Pierre, on their honeymoon, riding bikes given to them as
a wedding present by Marie's cousin.

MARIE CURIE

"NOTHING IN LIFE IS TO BE FEARED.
IT IS ONLY TO BE UNDERSTOOD."

PHILIP STEELE

CONTENTS

A WARSAW CHILDHOOD

1

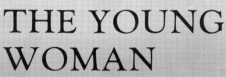

THE YOUNG WOMAN

2

PARTNERSHIP
OF GENIUS

3

THE FINAL
STRUGGLE

4

A WARSAW CHILDHOOD

1

Little Maria

Freta Street was at the heart of the old city of Warsaw, in Poland. Number 16 was a fine building, with an iron balcony at the front. It housed a small private school for girls, which was very well thought of. Everyone admired its young headmistress, a former pupil of the school called Bronislawa Sklodowska.

She and her husband, Wladislaw Sklodowski, lived in an apartment behind the classrooms, where the chatter and laughter of the girls could always be heard during school hours.

The couple's own children could make quite a lot of noise too. The eldest was a girl called Zofia, nicknamed 'Zosia', who had been born in 1862. The boy, Józef (or Jozio), was one year younger. Then there were two little girls, Bronislawa (Bronia, born in 1865) and Helena (Hela, born in 1866). All had fair hair and were lively and clever children. On 7 November 1867, the youngest daughter was born. Her parents called her Maria Salomea.

Previous page: Freta Street in the old part of Warsaw. Maria was born in an apartment here.

Right: Not far from Freta Street stood a tall column in memory of Zygmunt III. This king of Poland and Sweden had invaded Russia in 1609. By the 1800s, however, it was the Russians who ruled in Warsaw.

1860
Wladislaw Sklodowski marries Bronislawa Boguska.

1864
A Polish uprising against Russian rule is defeated.

Left: The Sklodowski children, from left to right – Zosia, the eldest; Hela; Maria, who was soon nicknamed 'Manya'; Jozio, the only boy; and Bronia.

What's in a name?

Maria Salomea Sklodowska had one grandmother named Maria and another named Salomea. 'Maria' had always been a special name in Poland, where many Catholics were devoted to the Virgin Mary, the mother of Jesus Christ. And why Sklodowska? The male version of Polish surnames ends in '-i', but the female in '-a'.

Like the other children, the new arrival was given a nickname, 'Manya'.

Maria's parents were interesting and intelligent people. Bronislawa was a devout Catholic, but her husband was not so religious. He was a scientist and a teacher of physics. Both parents came from families of high social standing, although they were never wealthy.

At that time, Poland was under foreign rule, and Warsaw was governed by Russia (see pages 14–15). Bronislawa and Wladislaw were nationalists, and they longed to see Poland ruling itself.

18 February 1867

The surgeon Joseph Lister first uses antiseptic during an operation, to prevent infection.

7 November 1867

Maria Salomea Slodowska is born at Freta Street in Warsaw.

··

Baby Maria did not remain in Freta Street for long. In 1868 her father was appointed physics teacher and assistant head of a boys' secondary school on Novolipki Street, in western Warsaw. The school was a long, low building set behind railings, with lilac trees growing in the courtyard. The headmaster was a Russian called Ivanov. He made sure that all lessons were taught in the Russian language, and not in Polish. Wladislaw did not like his new boss and found it difficult to hide his own nationalist feelings.

The job came with an apartment, and so the whole family moved to this new home. The rooms were furnished in the style of that time, with red velvet and dark polished wood. On the wall of Wladislaw's study, a barometer recorded air pressure and changing weather conditions. Little Maria was fascinated by this scientific instrument.

Left: Buildings in the historical centre of Warsaw, where the Sklodowski family lived until 1868, when they had to move to the west of the city.

1868
Wladislaw Sklodowski becomes assistant head at Novolipki Street High School.

1868
Bronislawa Sklodowska gives up her job at Freta Street.

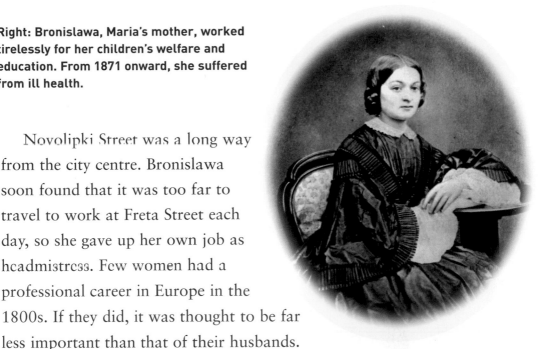

Right: Bronislawa, Maria's mother, worked tirelessly for her children's welfare and education. From 1871 onward, she suffered from ill health.

Novolipki Street was a long way from the city centre. Bronislawa soon found that it was too far to travel to work at Freta Street each day, so she gave up her own job as headmistress. Few women had a professional career in Europe in the 1800s. If they did, it was thought to be far less important than that of their husbands.

Bronislawa decided to teach Zosia and Józef at home. All the children were very bright, especially Maria. She learned to ask questions and to read at an early age. The little children loved to play with wooden bricks and to cut out pictures from magazines and paste them together. They played outside in the playground, too, but were happiest at the end of the summer term, when they could leave the city to stay with relatives in the countryside.

Mend my shoe

When money was short, Bronislawa Sklodowska decided to learn how to make and repair shoes for her children. She bought and cut out the leather, and stitched and hammered. She was a practical woman and never ashamed to turn her hand to hard work. Maria grew up with the same sense of the importance of hard work.

1870
France and Prussia are at war. Prussia is victorious.

1871
Bronislawa begins to feel ill.

Troubled Times

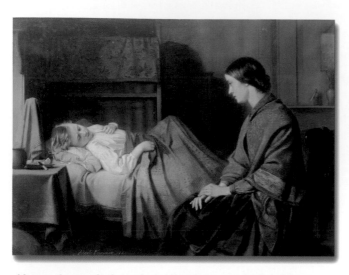

Above: A worried mother sits by her sick daughter's bed. In 1874 Maria's sister Zosia caught typhus and died. The Sklodowski family was heartbroken.

In 1871 Maria's mother, Bronislawa, became pale and began to lose weight. She coughed and coughed. The doctors said she was suffering from tuberculosis, a disease of the lungs.

Before 1882, when the German scientist Robert Koch discovered the germ that causes tuberculosis, people did not understand how the illness was passed on from one person to another. Bronislawa may have caught tuberculosis by breathing in germs while she nursed her brother-in-law, Przemislaw, who died from the disease.

In 1872 Bronislawa was sent abroad. Doctors believed that a change of climate, fresh air and rest would be the best treatment. She travelled with her eldest daughter, Zosia, first to a health resort in the Austrian Alps, then on to Nice in the south of France. Zosia was sent to a French school, where she did very well. Sadly, Bronislawa did not get better. Back in Poland, the other Sklodowski children missed their mother and sister dreadfully. Bronislawa's sister Ludwika (Aunt Lucia) did her best to help out in the home.

1872
Bronislawa Sklodowska leaves for Austria and France.

1874
Maria's sister Zosia dies of typhus.

Left: Wladislaw Sklodowski later wrote a poem in which he said that his wife's death turned his whole world 'into a cemetery'.

To make things worse, in 1873 their father lost his post as assistant head at the high school. He had always been distrusted by the Russians. The Sklodowskis now had to move to a new home, which Wladislaw turned into a small boarding school. It was here that Bronislawa and Zosia returned in the autumn of that year.

With the house full of schoolboys, the rooms were overcrowded. Another disease broke out in 1874. It was typhus, a terrible illness spread by fleas and lice. Both Zosia and Bronia became sick, and Zosia died.

Bronislawa, still ill with tuberculosis herself, was devastated. In 1876 she went to a health resort called Salzbrunn, in Germany, for another rest, but her spirit was broken. She died on 8 May 1878, having told the children how much she loved them. Maria never recovered from the grief of these years. She suffered greatly from the loss of a mother's love just as she was beginning to grow up.

Consumption

In the 1800s tuberculosis was often called 'consumption' because it consumed and destroyed the body. Today, we call it TB. It is a deadly disease that produces lumps on human tissue, especially in the lungs. In 1898 Maria's sister Bronia opened a treatment centre for TB sufferers in Poland.

1876
Alexander Graham Bell invents the telephone.

8 May 1878
Maria's mother, Bronislawa, dies of tuberculosis.

Maria's Poland

In the Middle Ages, Poland had been a strong kingdom. However, in the 1700s neighbouring countries became more powerful and began to seize Polish lands. In 1772 Prussia (a German kingdom) took the northwest; Russia occupied the northeast; and Austria, the southwest. In 1793 Prussia and Russia grabbed even more, and by 1795 all of central Poland had been swallowed up. Poland had ceased to exist on the map. During the Napoleonic Wars (1805–15), Napoleon attacked Russia and Prussia and created the Duchy of Warsaw. After Napoleon's defeat in 1815, this area returned to Russian and Prussian rule. In 1830 there was an uprising against the Russians, but it was put down. Maria's grandfather Józef Sklodowski fought in this rebellion. Other rebellions occurred in 1846, 1863 and 1864, but they also failed.

Below: Poland's borders have changed a great deal through history. After 1772 Poland was divided up between its neighbours no fewer than three times. It remained under foreign rule for more than a century.

Baltic Sea

PRUSSIA

RUSSIA

Gdansk

Minsk

Berlin

Szczuki

Kepa

Poznan

Warsaw

RUSSIAN POLAND

P O L A N D

Katowice

Skalbmierz

Krakow

Tatra Mountains

Prague

AUSTRIA

Vienna

▫	RUSSIAN POLAND
▫	RUSSIA
▪	PRUSSIA
▫	AUSTRIA

Border before partition ——
Modern border ——

Left: A band of poorly armed Polish rebels stand watch during the rebellion of 1863. Russian troops treated captives very harshly.

RUSSIAN RULE

When Maria was a girl, the ruler of Poland was the Russian emperor, or tsar. Russian school inspectors always made sure that Polish pupils knew his name: Alexander II (left). When the tsar was killed by Russian revolutionaries in 1881, Maria celebrated by dancing around the classroom with a friend.

Above: Tsar Alexander II inspects a troop of Russian soldiers. At the time, the Russian army was very strong and brutally put down any Polish revolt. Polish nationalist rebels either fled to France, like Maria's uncle Zdzislaw, or were captured and sent to a remote part of Russia called Siberia, like her uncle Henryk. Some Poles gave up the idea of armed uprising, declaring that they could win back respect and political power through hard work and education. They were known as 'positivists', and Maria shared their beliefs.

Top of the Class

Maria's parents did not believe that children should only learn in the classroom. Every game and every walk in the country was turned into a lesson. The children learned about the weather and nature, about science and maths, and about Polish history. They learned several languages too, as Maria's parents could also speak Russian, French and English.

When it came to school, Wladislaw and Bronislawa (when she was still alive) demanded that their children work very hard. Maria did not need to be told. She loved learning and reading, and had a very good memory.

Maria's first formal lessons were at the old Freta Street school where her mother had been headmistress. When Maria was six years old, she and her sister Hela were sent to a school nearer home. It was a private school run by a kind and clever woman called Jadwiga Sikorska. The children wore blue uniforms. Because Maria was very clever and hard-working, she was placed in a class with older children, together with her sister Hela.

Left: Schooling in Europe during the 1870s was often strict. Even small children had to learn long lists of facts or poems by heart and recite them before the class.

1878
Revolution stirs in Russia. Many Russian activists are exiled to Siberia.

Spring and summer 1878
Maria is grief-stricken over the death of her mother.

> *'She [Maria] always had her own opinion, which she knew how to defend.'*
>
> Helena (Hela) Sklodowska, Maria's sister

The school had two curricula. The official one was for the Russian government inspectors, and included Russian language and history. The unofficial curriculum was a Polish one. When the inspectors arrived, Maria was often the child chosen to be questioned in Russian because she spoke the language so well. When the inspectors left, the staff and pupils could relax and speak Polish again, but the arrangement was a strain on both the children and the teachers.

Jadwiga took good care of Maria and Hela. Bronislawa had died in the girls' first year at this school, and Maria had become very quiet and was clearly suffering a great deal. Jadwiga became so worried that, at the end of the school year of 1878, she went to speak to Maria's father. 'It might be wise to keep her down a year, so that she is with girls her own age,' she said.

Wladislaw would have none of it. He thought that Maria needed a new challenge to take her mind off things. He decided to send her to a new school. Hela stayed with Jadwiga Sikorska.

A tale of two cities

Wladislaw Sklodowski enjoyed reading his favourite stories and poems to the children, and they loved to listen. One book Maria wanted to hear over and over again was *A Tale of Two Cities*, by the English author Charles Dickens. It was an exciting story about the French Revolution and was set in Paris and London. As it happened, Maria's own life also became 'a tale of two cities' – Warsaw and Paris.

Summer 1878
Jadwiga Sikorska expresses concern over Maria's well-being.

Summer 1878
Maria's father decides to send her to a new school.

Afternoon treats

Maria's best friend at school, Kazia, was the daughter of a librarian who worked for a wealthy man called Count Zamoyski. Kazia lived in an apartment at his palace, and Maria liked to stop off there on her way home from school. She and Kazia would enjoy a snack of lemonade or chocolate ice cream.

Maria was entered at Gymnasium Number Three, a government secondary school that was housed in a former convent in the centre of Warsaw. The school was run in the Russian way and many of the teachers were very anti-Polish. It was not the sort of school that Maria's father admired, but, if Maria succeeded there, she would gain a diploma. This might give her the chance of further studies at a university.

Without the company of her sister Hela, Maria was lonely at the new school. Luckily, she soon made friends with another girl in her class, Kazia Przyboroska. At the time, Maria seemed happy enough with the school. Later in her life, however, she criticized the teaching, particularly the basic level of its science education. Some of Maria's teachers found her too strong-willed and did not like her.

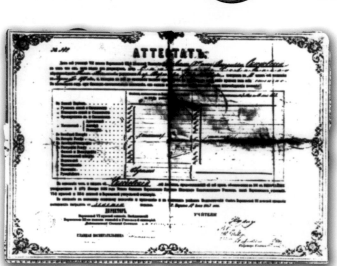

Above: Maria's graduation certificate from the Russian secondary school confirmed that she was a star pupil.

Autumn 1878	1881
Maria is sent to Gymnasium Number Three in central Warsaw.	When the Russian tsar Alexander II is killed, Maria and Kazia dance for joy.

Left: At the age of 16 Maria was a serious-looking girl. Her curly hair was pulled back from her forehead for tidiness.

Everyone agreed that Maria was a brilliant student, and on 12 June 1883, aged 15, she graduated from secondary school. She was declared best in her class and awarded a gold medal. Her brother and sisters were also very successful in their studies, and their father was proud of them all.

What would Maria do next? Most girls of her age would soon be thinking of marriage, but Maria's mind was on education. Might she become a teacher or even go to college? Warsaw University did not accept women as students, but she would be able to study in St Petersburg, in Russia, or else in Paris – if only she had the money.

At this point, the years of strain began to show. Maria had concentrated on her work and had not grieved properly for Zosia and her mother. Without the distraction of schoolwork, she became depressed and very withdrawn. She ate very little, and chose to lie on her bed with the curtains drawn.

12 June 1883
Maria graduates from secondary school with a gold medal.

Late summer 1883
Maria suffers from a period of depression.

THE YOUNG
WOMAN

Sweet Sixteen

Wladislaw Sklodowski eventually decided that something had to be done for his depressed daughter. He sent Maria off to the countryside to recover and relax. The year that followed was one of the happiest of her life.

Both sides of Maria's family belonged to the social class known in Polish as *slachta*: people who owned manor houses with country estates. Many of Maria's relatives were slachta, so there were plenty of places for her to stay.

Maria's train took her south to Zwola, where she visited her mother's brothers, Henryk and Wladislaw. Their two households were full of dogs, music, books and laughter. She enjoyed all sorts of childish games, played shuttlecock, sketched and rode horses.

The winter of 1883–84 was spent in Skalbmierz, in the foothills of the Tatra Mountains, with her uncle Zdzislaw, a lawyer. His wife, another Maria, was thought to be rather shocking. She smoked and had no time for housekeeping. She set up a lacemaking school and a furniture workshop.

Above: Dancing and music became a way for Polish people to express their national identity in the 1800s. At one time, the Russians even banned Poles from dancing in national costume.

Previous page: Maria in 1891, when she finally fulfilled her dream of studying at college.

Early autumn 1883
Maria visits her uncles Henryk and Wladislaw.

November 1883
Maria travels to Skalbmierz, to stay with Uncle Zdzislaw and Aunt Maria.

Above: Maria loved going on sleigh rides at Skalbmierz. She would travel with her friends through the snow from one ball to another, accompanied by fiddle music.

Dance the mazurka!

Maria had taken dancing classes and could now dance quite well. At Skalbmierz, she went to costumed balls where the young men dressed up in the folk costume of the region. The mazurka, a very lively Polish dance in triple time, was Maria's favourite.

In the company of her cousins, Maria enjoyed walking in the mountains and soon looked fit, healthy and happy. She was turning into an attractive young woman.

After returning to Warsaw that July, Maria and her sister Hela were immediately invited to stay with a former pupil of their mother's, the Comtesse de Fleurie. Her beautiful house and estate was at Kepa, to the northeast of Warsaw. There the young people played practical jokes on each other, swam, boated in the sunshine and ate cherries. It was a magical time for Maria.

July 1884
Hela and Maria are invited to Kepa.

1885
The Frenchman Louis Pasteur develops a vaccination against rabies.

A Governess

Maria returned to Warsaw at the end of the summer. Her father had given up his little boarding school and had moved into a smaller apartment. He did find some other teaching work, but it only paid enough money to help his son, Józef, study medicine. The trouble was, both Bronia and Maria also dreamed of studying.

Bronia and Maria often talked about the future. The two sisters became very close to each other. They wanted to make something of themselves and help their native Poland, too. They supported the positivists – thinkers who called for progress through education and science. Bronia and Maria wanted to see the workers and the peasants in the countryside receive schooling, not just the middle and upper classes.

Left: The Polish positivists demanded education for the poor, such as these peasants, and equal rights for women. Bronia and Maria were keen supporters.

Autumn 1885
Maria and Bronia give private lessons for pupils.

1885
Karl Benz develops the first petrol-powered automobile.

Left: Maria (left) and Bronia both wanted to study in Paris, but how could they afford it? Their father was ashamed that he could not raise the money himself.

The positivists wanted women to get the same chances in life as men, in education and in the workplace. They also wanted to see the Catholic Church become less powerful in Poland. Both girls, like their father, were now much more interested in scientific research than in religion.

Bronia and Maria made money by teaching private pupils at home. In December 1885 Maria became a governess for a rich Warsaw family, but she hated them. Her new employers were wasteful and stingy at the same time, and they put on airs.

In the end, it was Maria who worked out a plan to make her and Bronia's dreams come true. She would become a governess in the country and send half her wages to Bronia. This would make it possible for her sister to study medicine in Paris. Once Bronia had qualified, she would become a doctor and pay for Maria to come and study in Paris.

The Flying University

In 1882 a secret academy for women was founded in Warsaw. Despite attempts by the authorities to break it up, about 1,000 women had joined up by 1890, including Bronia and Maria Sklodowska. It became known as the 'Flying University'.

December 1885
Maria becomes a governess in Warsaw.

1886
Warsaw's secret academy for women is renamed the 'Flying University'.

Above: The house at Szczuki was pleasant enough, but the surrounding countryside was flat, dull farmland. Mr Zorawski managed a large country estate, and the house was next to a sugar beet factory.

On New Year's Day 1886, Maria set out for her new job as governess. Her home was to be that of the Zorawski family, at Szczuki, about 63 miles (100 km) to the north of Warsaw.

Some of the Zorawski children were away at school in Warsaw, and there was also a six-year-old and a baby. Maria only taught Andzia, a ten-year-old girl, and the eldest daughter, Bronka. Bronka was 18, much the same age as Maria herself. The two became good friends.

The Zorawskis treated their governess well enough, but never quite as an equal. Maria spent her spare time reading and studying science. With nearly half her wages going to her sister Bronia, she had little money to buy new dresses.

January 1886	1888
Maria goes to work as a governess with the Zorawski family.	Wladislaw Sklodowski becomes director of a reform school.

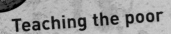

Teaching the poor

Maria and Bronka Zorawska set up a school in the kitchen at Szczuki for 20 poor children whose parents worked on the estate. This was illegal. If the Russian authorities had found out, the young women would have been imprisoned or sent to Siberia.

However, when the Zorawskis' eldest son, Kazimierz, came home from Warsaw University, he was charmed by the young governess, as she was by him. They soon fell in love. Eventually, Kazimierz told his parents that he wished to marry Maria. The Zorawskis were horrified. Their son could not marry someone as lowly as a mere governess! Maria was far too poor and her family owned no land.

Kazimierz did not know what to do. Eventually, he obeyed his parents, leaving Maria very deeply hurt. She continued in her job, however, because she – and Bronia – needed the money.

At last, in 1889, Maria left the Zorawski home. She briefly took another appointment as governess with a wealthy family named Fuchs. Then, in March 1890, she received an invitation from Bronia: 'Come to Paris next year.'

Circumstances at home had changed, and the family now had money. In 1888 Maria's father was appointed director of a reform school for young offenders outside Warsaw. It was not a pleasant job, but it paid well. He had been able to send money to Bronia in Paris and to start paying off Bronia's debt to Maria.

Above: Kazimierz Zorawski was a handsome young student. Maria was deeply upset when his family stopped the two from marrying.

1889
Maria leaves Szczuki and joins the Fuchs family on the Baltic Sea coast.

March 1890
Bronia invites Maria to join her in Paris.

Student Days

Now that Maria's big chance had come, she could not make up her mind. Should she really go to Paris? And if she did, what would she study?

Surely, her subject had to be physics? Having returned to Warsaw, Maria was already spending time in the laboratory at the Museum of Industry and Agriculture, where her cousin Józef Boguski was director. She loved setting up experiments using scientific equipment and trying to get the correct result.

Toward the end of 1891, Maria made up her mind at last and she boarded the train to Paris. When she arrived, she registered to study physics at the university college of the Sorbonne, under the French name of Marie Sklowodska. Marie she was to be, from now on.

Above: After moving to Paris in 1891, Marie spent many years in France. She also made trips to several other countries in western Europe.

At first, she stayed with her sister on the Rue d'Allemagne. Bronia had already graduated, one of only three women out of 1,000 medical students. Bronia had also married while in Paris.

Bronia's new husband was a doctor called Kazimierz Dluski.

1890–91	November 1891
Maria is in Warsaw. She experiments in her cousin's laboratory.	Maria travels to Paris. She becomes known as Marie.

Left: When Marie arrived in Paris, it was the most fashionable and artistic city in the world. It was also a city of science and technology.

He had left Poland for political reasons. He was a socialist and believed that complete economic change was the only way to create a fair society. He disagreed with the idealistic reforms suggested by the positivists.

Marie found it hard to get down to her studies. The apartment was always busy, full of arguments and laughter, and friends talking in Polish. Marie needed to practise her French until it was perfect, and she had little time for parties or chatter. She decided to rent her own apartment, in the student district of Paris, known as the Latin Quarter.

Marie moved several times in the years that followed, from one cold and threadbare attic room in Paris to another. In the summers, she would go back to Poland to see her family or take holidays with them.

Naughty Nineties?

Poor artists, poets and students flocked to Paris in the 1890s. It was an exciting place, with bars, dance halls and costumed balls. Shocking dances such as the can-can were performed on stage. Marie had no time for any of this. She was determined to get on with her work.

1891
Marie lives with Bronia and Kazimierz Dluski.

1892
Marie lives in a small apartment at Number 3, Rue Flatters.

Science for the Future

During Marie's lifetime, many people started to believe that science was the key to human progress. Scientists like Marie were often idealistic. Some refused to patent their inventions (register them as their own private work). Instead, they believed that their research was for the good of all humanity, not just one individual, one company or one country. The public began to hope that science might solve all the world's problems, but they were soon disappointed. However, many great scientists were alive at the same time as Marie. These included Albert Einstein, who improved our understanding of the universe; Dimitri Mendeleyev, who created a system that we still use today for cataloguing the basic elements; and Wilhelm Röntgen, whose discovery of x-rays revolutionized modern medicine.

Background: The Sorbonne in Paris had once been famous for its religious studies. By the 1890s it had become a centre of scientific research. Its professors included the physicist Gabriel Lippmann (1845–1921), whose work made colour photography possible.

Below: Dimitri Mendeleyev (1834–1907) was a Russian chemist. Marie's cousin Józef Boguski once worked as his assistant. Mendeleyev studied the elements (basic substances that contain no other materials, such as carbon and oxygen). Mendeleyev made a chart or table that listed them – this is known as the periodic table of elements. Today, we know that there are at least 110 elements.

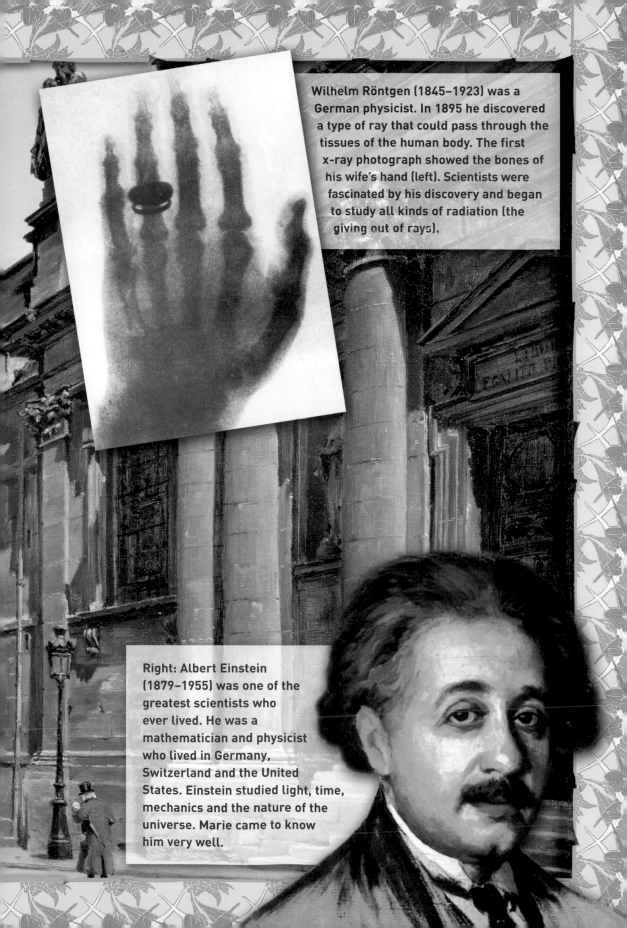

Wilhelm Röntgen (1845–1923) was a German physicist. In 1895 he discovered a type of ray that could pass through the tissues of the human body. The first x-ray photograph showed the bones of his wife's hand (left). Scientists were fascinated by his discovery and began to study all kinds of radiation (the giving out of rays).

Right: Albert Einstein (1879–1955) was one of the greatest scientists who ever lived. He was a mathematician and physicist who lived in Germany, Switzerland and the United States. Einstein studied light, time, mechanics and the nature of the universe. Marie came to know him very well.

Hard Work

Above: This simple sketch of Marie was made by a fellow student during her early days at college.

There were 2,000 students studying sciences at the Sorbonne, but only 23 of them were women. Marie Sklodowska was the first young woman ever to study physics there.

Everyone was polite to Marie, but few of the male students or professors took her seriously. They believed that no woman could ever be as clever or as hard-working as a man. She was determined to prove them wrong. She worked very hard and ate too little. She had no money to spare and rarely relaxed or enjoyed herself.

The examinations for Marie's licence, or degree, were in July 1893. As the date approached, she became more and more nervous. She need not have been. Not only did she pass, but she rated first of all the students, a truly amazing accomplishment.

When Marie returned to Poland for the summer holidays, her family was very proud. So too were many campaigners for women's education. One of them, Jadwiga Dydynska, called for Marie to receive a scholarship. She was successful, and Marie was offered 600 rubles, which was enough for her to live on for 15 months. This made it possible for her to take a second degree – in mathematics. In the summer of 1894 she passed, finishing second of all the students. Typically, Marie felt she should have worked harder and finished first.

1893
New Zealand is the first country in the world to give women the vote.

July 1893
Marie receives her physics degree at the Sorbonne.

Above: *Woman on a Lawn* was painted by the French artist Camille Pissarro (1830–1903). On some Sundays, Marie left the city centre to enjoy fresh air. Throughout her life, she loved to relax by visiting the countryside.

Marie was now a graduate twice over. This should have been the time for her to return to Poland. However, she had been offered work – and had met a very interesting man.

Paris in the spring

Marie took little notice of anything besides her studies. However, when spring sunshine arrived and warmed her room, her spirits rose. Sometimes, she would take a trip out of Paris for the day. In 1893 she wrote to her father of green shoots, lilac and apple blossom. The French climate was milder than that of her native Poland.

Summer 1893
Marie is awarded the Alexandrovitch Scholarship of 600 rubles.

Summer 1894
Marie receives a second degree, in mathematics.

PARTNERSHIP OF GENIUS

3

Marie and Pierre

Marie had new work to be getting on with. Gabriel Lippmann, one of her professors at the Sorbonne, had set up a project for her. Her task was to study the magnetism of steel. The French Society for the Encouragement of Industry was prepared to offer her a grant of 600 francs for this work. This was enough to pay for food and the rent of a tiny apartment for a year.

There was just one problem. Lippmann's laboratory was overcrowded and Marie needed more space. One day, a couple Marie knew from Poland called upon her in Paris. The husband, Professor Józef Kowalski, suggested that Marie contact a friend of his for advice. His name was Pierre Curie.

Pierre was 35 years old and worked in Paris for the School of Industrial Physics and Chemistry. He found a small space where Marie could work.

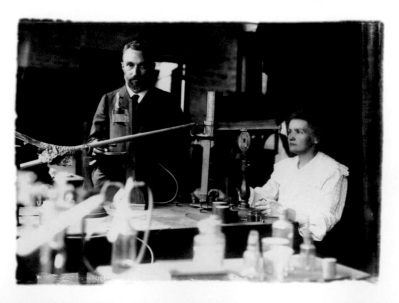

Previous page: Pierre and Marie Curie with their eldest daughter, Irène, in about 1899.

Left: Marie and Pierre in the laboratory. It was a love of science that first brought them together. They shared the same interest in physics and worked together very well. Pierre's first gift to Marie was a scientific book he had written.

1894
Marie is offered a grant to study the magnetism of steel.

1894
Marie meets Pierre Curie.

Pierre was a brilliant scientist. He had invented many useful instruments and was an expert in magnetism. He and his brother, Jacques, had studied quartz crystals and electricity. In the next century, this line of research would lead others to develop items such as quartz watches and microphones.

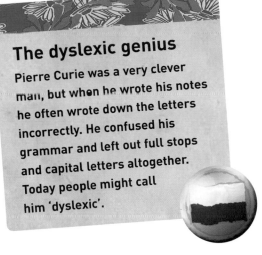

The dyslexic genius

Pierre Curie was a very clever man, but when he wrote his notes he often wrote down the letters incorrectly. He confused his grammar and left out full stops and capital letters altogether. Today people might call him 'dyslexic'.

After her failed romance with Kazimierz Zorawski, Marie had never imagined that she could fall in love again. Fifteen years before, Pierre's only love had died. Marie and Pierre had both come to the conclusion that love would only cause heartache – and that it was rather silly anyway. Yet these two people did fall in love, against their own better judgment. They were perfectly suited – they were both intelligent and thought of little but science. They were also practical people who disliked fuss.

Pierre and Marie had first met in the spring of 1894. When Marie went off to Poland for her summer holiday that year, she still was not sure of her feelings, even when Pierre sent her love letters. However, a year later, she wrote to her family and friends from Paris to tell them that she and Pierre were to be married.

Left: The Curie brothers Jacques and Pierre (right) stand behind their parents, Dr Eugène Curie and his wife, Sophie-Claire Depouilly. The Curies had a similar land-owning background to Marie's own family in Poland.

1895
Wilhelm Röntgen discovers x-rays.

Spring 1895
Pierre Curie presents a paper on magnetism at the Sorbonne to earn his doctorate.

On 26 July 1895, Marie and Pierre took a train from central Paris to the suburb of Sceaux, where Pierre's family lived. There they were married, in a simple ceremony at the town hall. Marie wore a navy blue suit and a light blue blouse. It was a very happy day. Marie's father and her sister Hela came from Warsaw. Bronia and Kazimierz Dluski were there too. Roses bloomed in the garden; there were bottles of champagne, and, after lunch, a game of boules (similar to lawn bowling).

Pierre and Marie had been given two new bicycles. They set off on these for their honeymoon, taking them on a train and then enjoying a cycling tour of the rocky coastline of Brittany in northwest France.

Back in Paris, Marie and Pierre rented an apartment on the Rue de la Glacière. Marie managed the household and kept the accounts. Typically, she also took on more study courses and trained as a teacher, and she also had to finish her research into steel and put together her findings. Pierre, now a doctor of science, was doing more research on crystals and was giving lectures on electricity.

In 1897 Marie was expecting a child. She did not feel well and so took time off in Brittany. By 12 September she was back in Paris, where the baby girl was delivered by her father-in-law, who was a doctor. The child was named Irène.

Marie enjoyed observing her baby's growth as if it was an experiment.

Moving pictures

Cinema was pioneered by two French brothers, Auguste and Louis Lumière. They showed the world's first film on 28 December 1895, at the Grand Café on the Boulevard des Capucines in Paris. It was in Paris the following year that Pierre and Marie Curie saw a film for the first time.

26 July 1895
Marie marries Pierre Curie in Sceaux, a suburb of Paris.

1895
Louis and Auguste Lumière invent the motion picture camera.

She found it difficult to work and care for the baby as well, and became anxious. When Pierre's mother died two weeks after the birth, his father offered to help them out. All four moved to a new house on the Boulevard Kellermann.

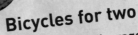

Bicycles for two

Cycling was all the rage in the 1890s. Bicycles gave people a new freedom to travel and kept them fit, too. Pierre and Marie Curie became keen cyclists, touring the Brittany and Auvergne regions of France. Cycling needed practical clothing, and old-fashioned people were shocked to see young women such as Marie dressed in culottes (loose trousers) instead of a dress.

Left: Ready for the road! Pierre and Marie prepare to leave for their honeymoon in July 1895. They proudly show off their new bicycles, bought by a cousin as a wedding gift. Their honeymoon was a cycling tour of the beautiful coastline of Brittany.

12 September 1897
Marie gives birth to a baby girl, Irène.

27 September 1897
Pierre's mother dies. His father moves in with Pierre and Marie.

In the Laboratory

In 1896 Wilhelm Röntgen's discovery of x-rays became known to the public. Scientists everywhere were fascinated. They soon discovered that x-rays were like rays of light, only with a shorter wavelength (see page 61). Scientists started to study other kinds of rays, or radiation, too.

The French physicist Henri Becquerel became interested in the rays given out by an element called uranium. Marie needed a new area of research in order to earn a doctorate from the Sorbonne. She decided to follow up on Becquerel's work.

Becquerel suggested that uranium rays created currents of electricity. This was confirmed later by a Scottish scientist called Lord Kelvin. Marie decided to investigate and study these electrical currents. They were tiny, but Pierre perfected the equipment needed to measure them.

Marie also began to study other materials that gave out rays, such as thorium and compounds that contained uranium. One of these was called pitchblende.

Right: Henri Becquerel was a difficult man to work with, but his discoveries about radiation meant that he shared the glory of the Curies' discoveries. Here he wears the uniform of the French Academy of Sciences.

February 1898
Marie starts to measure the radioactivity of pitchblende.

March 1898
Pierre gives up his work on crystals and works with Marie.

Radioactive!

In July 1898 Marie invented a new word to describe the kind of radiation she was measuring. It was not like other kinds of radiation, and its cause was as yet unknown. She called it 'radioactivity', a term that has been used ever since.

This ore was mined in what is now the German–Czech border region.

The pitchblende samples Marie tested gave off the most powerful radiation of all. This was odd, because their uranium had already been taken out, for use in manufacturing glass and pottery. Surely the samples of this compound must contain some unknown elements that were the source of the rays?

The Curies tried to discover these unknown elements using a spectroscope. By this method, substances were heated and the rays of light they gave out were passed through a glass prism, which broke the light rays up into different colours. This should have helped to identify the mystery elements, but the Curies were unable to get clear results. In March and April 1898 Marie wrote reports that were presented to the French Academy of Sciences. Finally, on 18 July, a third report identified an unknown element as 'polonium', named in honour of Poland. By the end of that year, Marie had identified another element. She called it 'radium', from the Latin word for 'ray'.

> *'All my mind was centred on my studies. I divided my time between courses, experimental work, and study in the library. In the evening I worked in my room, sometimes very late into the night. All that I saw and learned was a new delight to me.'*
> **Autobiographical Notes, Marie Curie**

July 1898
The element polonium is identified and named after Poland.

December 1898
The element radium is identified.

Above: A photograph from 1898 shows Marie and Pierre in their laboratory. It was here that they discovered polonium and radium.

Although Marie and Pierre had identified two 'new' elements, these still had to be isolated – separated from all the other compounds in the ore. Radium was very radioactive indeed, and it turned out to be the easier of the two to isolate. Even so, it was still a very difficult job.

The space that Pierre had found for Marie was no longer big enough. She was given an old glass shed at Pierre's college. This was freezing in winter and hot in summer. Marie also needed plenty of pitchblende. More than ten tonnes of pitchblende, with the uranium already extracted, was brought all the way from Austria. It was still covered in the pine needles from the forest floor where the ore had been dumped.

Once in the laboratory, the pitchblende was treated with chemicals to break it down. The most radioactive substances that came out of this were then treated in turn. In the end, it was hoped, only radium would be left. So Marie boiled up pitchblende in a huge cauldron, stirring it with a metal rod.

The Curies were racking their brains over the big question. Why were some elements radioactive and some not? The two scientists were lost in their work.

May 1902

Wladislaw Sklodowski dies in Poland, age 70.

July 1902

Marie at last isolates radium in the form of a compound known as a salt.

They hardly remembered to eat, and at times little Irène saw more of her grandfather than her parents.

The Curies needed more income. Marie took on extra work as head of physics at the École Normale Supérieure at Sèvres, outside Paris, a leading college for the training of women teachers. Pierre was offered a job as professor in Geneva, Switzerland, but he decided to turn it down. The Curies did take some time off and enjoyed holidays in Brittany and in Poland. Sadly, Marie's father, Wladislaw, died in May 1902.

The glow show

Materials with large amounts of radium glowed in the dark. Marie and Pierre were delighted with this discovery; they had no idea that it was deadly. They took no notice when they were 'burned' by radioactive materials. In fact, their whole workshop had been contaminated by radioactivity.

The Curies' work was greatly admired, but not all French scientists supported them – because Marie was a woman and Pierre made little effort to fit into the scientific world. Pierre applied to become a member of the Academy of Sciences in 1902, but was turned down. In July, Marie isolated a tiny amount of radium in the form of a salt. There was great public interest as the heating effect of radium suggested it could be a source of energy. The Curies' place in the history of science was certain.

Right: Pitchblende is a radioactive black ore. It contains a compound called uranium oxide, as well as lead, cerium, thallium, polonium and radium.

June 1903	November 1903
Marie is awarded a doctorate at the Sorbonne.	Marie, Pierre and Henri Becquerel win the Nobel Prize in physics.

Radioactivity and Atoms

Below: In 1899 Ernest Rutherford worked out that radium gave out two types of radiation. He called these alpha and beta particles, named after the first two letters of the Greek alphabet. In 1900 a third type was identified. It was later called gamma radiation after the third Greek letter.

Radioactivity was a puzzle. Where did these rays come from? One of the laws of physics was that energy, such as radiation, could not be created out of nothing. However, the elements that Marie Curie examined did not seem to be going through any kind of change, so how could they be creating energy? Could it be that the laws of physics were wrong? Or were the atoms of the element being affected by something else, perhaps some other kind of invisible ray? New Zealand scientist Ernest Rutherford (1871–1937) believed that the answer to the puzzle lay in the *structure* of the atom. At first, the Curies did not agree with him, but in the end they had to admit that he was right. Elements such as radium or polonium did not stay the same. They were in a very slow process of breaking down, or 'decaying'. That process of change made them give out rays.

ATOMIC PARTICLES

This image shows the structure of an atom. For most of the 1800s, scientists believed that atoms were the smallest existing part of any substance. However, in 1897 the English physicist J.J. Thomson discovered that they contained even smaller particles, which he called electrons. In 1911 Ernest Rutherford suggested that electrons travelled around a central core, or nucleus. Later, other particles that make up atoms were discovered, including protons and neutrons.

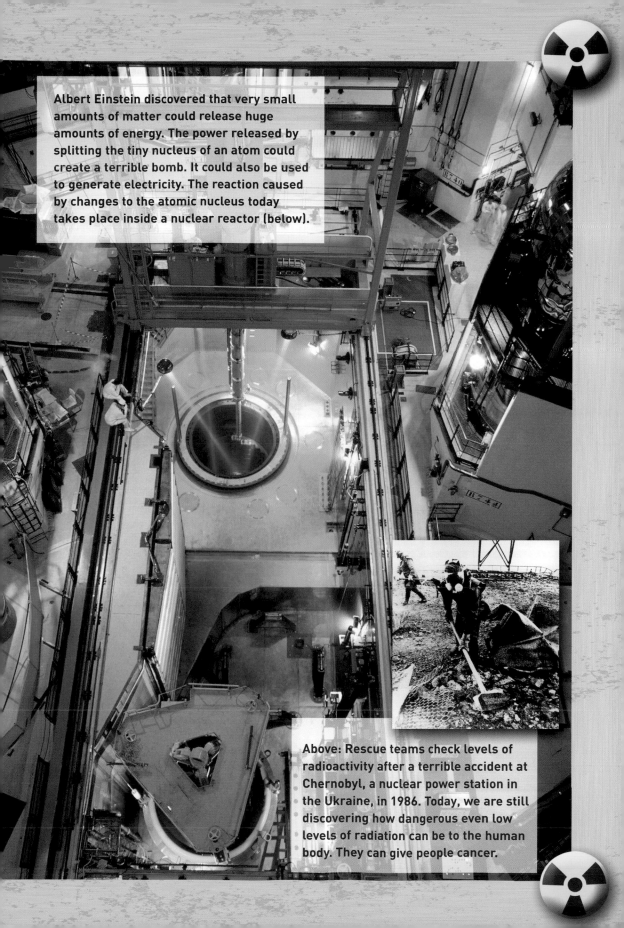

Albert Einstein discovered that very small amounts of matter could release huge amounts of energy. The power released by splitting the tiny nucleus of an atom could create a terrible bomb. It could also be used to generate electricity. The reaction caused by changes to the atomic nucleus today takes place inside a nuclear reactor (below).

Above: Rescue teams check levels of radioactivity after a terrible accident at Chernobyl, a nuclear power station in the Ukraine, in 1986. Today, we are still discovering how dangerous even low levels of radiation can be to the human body. They can give people cancer.

Triumph and Tragedy

In June 1903 Marie Curie presented her paper on radioactivity to the professors of the Sorbonne. She was made a doctor of physics, the first woman in France to achieve this honour.

Above: Marie (back row, third from left) poses with student teachers at Sèvres.

Marie's sister Bronia, who had returned to Poland with her husband, came back to Paris to join the family celebrations. That evening they were all invited to dinner with the physicist Paul Langevin and a surprise guest, another physicist working in the same field as Pierre and Marie: Ernest Rutherford.

In November, Marie Curie received an even greater honour: the Nobel Prize in physics. This was awarded jointly to her, to Pierre and to Henri Becquerel. It was still a man's world and Marie was nearly not included in the award. Everyone assumed that it must have been Pierre Curie who had done most of the work. Pierre always insisted that Marie be given the credit she deserved. In truth, both of them deserved the prize equally.

The Curies still wanted to lead a simple life, but they were now famous, and they did not like all the attention. Both had good jobs at the university.

December 1903
The Wright brothers make the world's first aeroplane flight at Kitty Hawk, North Carolina.

6 December 1904
Marie and Pierre's second daughter, Ève Denise Curie, is born.

The Nobel Prize

Alfred Nobel (1833–96) was a Swedish chemist who invented dynamite and other explosives. He decided to use his fortune to set up an award after his death. This prize would be given to people who had made advances in the sciences or in medicine, who had written great books or tried to bring about peace. The prizes were first awarded in 1901.

Pierre Curie was made a professor at the Sorbonne and Marie became the head of research. They had also made a deal with a factory owner called Armet de Lisle, to produce radium salts. What should happen next? There were so many difficult decisions to be made.

The Nobel awards ceremony was delayed, for Marie was pregnant again and not in the best of health. On 6 December 1904, Marie gave birth to a second daughter, Ève Denise Curie. In June 1905 Marie and Pierre finally travelled to Sweden to receive their award.

The next spring a terrible accident occurred. Pierre was walking in Paris, deep in thought and not paying attention. Possibly he was already becoming sick from the effects of radiation. He stepped into the road by a bridge, the Pont Neuf, and was knocked down by horses pulling a heavy wagon, which ran him over. He was killed.

Left: In 1905 Marie holds Ève, the chubby baby, while young Irène looks solemnly at the photographer.

1905
The physicist Albert Einstein publishes his theory of relativity.

18 April 1906
Pierre Curie is killed in an accident in Paris.

THE FINAL STRUGGLE

4

Desperation

It is hard to imagine Marie's grief when Pierre was killed. She was 39 years old, but it was just as if she was a child again, having lost her mother and sister. She became very depressed and, in this state, she was unable to offer much comfort to her own children.

Previous page: Marie Curie is photographed in 1930, at the age of 63.

Marie even became interested in spiritualism. Spiritualists believed that one could get in touch with the spirits of the dead. It was not at all scientific, but Marie was desperately missing Pierre. However, as usual, she tried to pull herself together through hard work. She was given Pierre's job as professor of physics at the Sorbonne and carried on working in the laboratory. Other laboratories were now conducting research on radium, and Marie set up a system of certification for them. Her manner was often prickly, and some scientists complained that she wanted to keep too much control over radium research. In 1910 she finally managed to isolate radium in the form of a metal.

Left: Paul Langevin (1872–1946; right) was himself a great scientist. He worked with Pierre Curie and with J.J. Thomson. Years later, Paul's grandson Michel would marry Marie's granddaughter, Helène.

1910
Marie Curie isolates radium in the form of a metal.

1910
Marie begins a love affair with Paul Langevin.

Left: The Solvay Conference, held in Brussels in 1911, brought together the world's greatest physicists, including Albert Einstein, Ernest Rutherford and Paul Langevin. Marie Curie, the only woman, sits at the front, talking to Henri Poincaré, the great mathematician and physicist.

Marie's daughters were educated with the children of other Sorbonne professors. The parents took turns teaching the children at home. Irène was brilliant at maths and science, while Ève showed a talent for music.

In 1910, Marie began a love affair with a married friend, Paul Langevin. There was a scandal in the press, which made Marie feel wretched. When male scientists behaved like this, no one said a word against them. Now, mobs were throwing stones at her house. The affair was broken off.

In 1911 the French Academy of Sciences turned Marie Curie down for membership because she was a woman. In the same year, she won a second Nobel Prize, this time for chemistry. Only one other person, the scientist Linus Pauling (1901–94), has ever won two Nobel Prizes. However, when they heard of her love affair, the Nobel committee asked Marie not to come to Sweden to accept her prize. Marie was furious. She insisted that her private life had nothing to do with her science – and went to the ceremony anyway.

Measure for measure

There was no standard unit of measurement for radioactivity. In 1910 the International Congress of Radiology and Electricity met in Brussels, Belgium, to decide what this should be. They agreed to call the new unit a 'curie'.

October 1911
The world's leading physicists meet at the Solvay Conference in Brussels.

November 1911
Marie Curie wins a second Nobel Prize, this time in chemistry.

Kill or Cure?

Shortly before his death in 1902, Wladislaw Sklodowski wrote to his daughter. 'It was a pity,' he said, 'that radium did not seem to have any practical uses.' However, within a few years some people were claiming that radium had miraculous powers and that it could cure all sorts of diseases, from arthritis (a stiffening of the joints) to mental problems. These claims were false and dangerous. Radioactivity damages the body and can cause cancers. Some of the people who used phony radium cures died a horrible death. As she got older, Marie Curie often complained of being tired. In reality, she was becoming sick from radiation.

Marie Curie hoped that radiation might be used to *cure* cancer. She began research into radium treatment, now known as radiotherapy. Radiation given in carefully measured doses can destroy cancers. After the 1930s medical treatments using radium and other radioactive materials, as well as x-rays, were used to fight cancer. Pellets or gold needles containing radium were inserted into cancerous growths. Today, radium is hardly ever used in radiotherapy. The most useful radiation comes from gamma rays given off by cobalt.

Above: This newspaper advertisement claims that radium can be used to treat grey hair, turning it back to its natural colour.

RADIUM v. GREY HAIR

Who'd Dream she was 50?

'Caradium' is NOT A DYE

Caradium

Right: Radium chic! The excitement over radium even influenced fashion. In this 1922 photograph, the American film star Gloria Swanson models a wig made of 'radium gray silk threads'.

Left: In the 1920s and 1930s advertisements claimed that hair lotions and face creams containing radium were good for you. In fact, the opposite was true. Tiny amounts of radium were put into tonics, toothpaste and shampoos. This face cream containing radium was supposed to give women a 'healthy glow'. Like many similar products, it used the name 'Curie', without Marie's permission.

CRÈME SCIENTIFIQUE

CURATIVE EMBELLISSANTE

THO-RADIA

à base de thorium et de radium selon la formule du
DOCTEUR ALFRED CURIE
EN VENTE EXCLUSIVEMENT CHEZ LES PHARMACIENS

Right: This advertisement from 1924 sells a product containing radium that can be used to produce long-lasting curls.

Our New Radium $5.00
Permanent Wave Beauty
COPYRIGHT
1924
P.W. CHERRY

Left: A cancer patient at a New York hospital receives radiation treatment, in about 1955. Radiotherapy is still used to treat cancer sufferers today.

War and Peace

From 1912 to 1913 Marie's children were being cared for by a Polish governess at a new apartment in Paris. Marie was feeling ill. She was having a nervous breakdown, brought on by the scandal caused by her love affair.

Marie went on a trip to the coast of southern England. Here, she was helped and nursed back to health by a woman called Hertha Ayrton, who was a scientist and campaigner for women's rights. Marie returned to Paris, where construction was beginning on a new Radium Institute.

In September 1914, at the start of World War I, German troops invaded Belgium and northeastern France. The French government left Paris for the southwestern city of Bordeaux. Marie travelled there by train, carrying her precious supply of radium with her. This could not fall into enemy hands.

Right: As World War I went on and on, millions of young men were killed and injured on the battlefields.

1912
Marie has a nervous breakdown.

1914
Construction begins on the Radium Institute in Paris.

Above: At the start of the war, Marie learned to drive. She converted a Renault truck into a mobile x-ray unit, which she drove from one hospital to another.

Radium was a valuable research resource that Marie hoped could be used for medical purposes.

Marie and her teenage daughter Irène wanted to save lives in this war. They fitted out x-ray trucks that used the vehicle's battery to power equipment inside. Marie often had to argue with generals and clerks in order to get these trucks to hospitals near the front lines. The x-rays were able to show the location of injuries, so that doctors could then operate with more precision. Irène helped tirelessly in hospitals in Belgium and France, while Ève stayed with her governess.

The United States entered World War I in 1917. Before American troops left for home at the end of the war in 1918, Marie trained many of their doctors in the use of the x-ray equipment she had developed.

In 1919 the map of Europe was redrawn once again. Poland was free at last, and this brought great joy to Marie and her family. Poland would have many more problems in the future, but for the moment it was an independent nation.

Les Petites Curie

The x-ray trucks sent to the battlefields of World War I became known as 'Little Curies' (in French, *'Petites Curie'*). Their operators took more than a million x-ray images and saved countless lives.

1914–18
World War I. Marie equips x-ray trucks to treat wounded soldiers.

1919
Poland becomes a free nation.

Left: Marie Curie meets the press in New York City. Journalists found Marie to be too shy and withdrawn when she spoke to them.

In the years after the war, Marie Curie received honours from universities around the world. Warsaw University made her a professor, although she was not expected to work there, and she was now director of the new Radium Institute in Paris. Once, Marie and Pierre had worked in old sheds and storerooms. Now she had modern laboratories and directed groups of researchers who were continuing and extending her work.

In 1920 Marie met an American journalist called Marie 'Missy' Meloney. Marie Curie needed to have more radium for her research. In 1921 Missy organized a fund-raising tour of the United States to pay for radium supplies.

Marie Curie travelled by ocean liner from Cherbourg, France, to New York, with Irène and Ève. Marie had always been shy and she hated the

> *'Madame Curie is not only a famous physicist: she is the greatest laboratory director I have ever known.'*
>
> **Professor Jean Baptiste Perrin (1870–1942), quoted in Ève Curie's biography of her mother**

1921
Marie Curie tours the United States.

1925
John Logie Baird transmits the first television pictures.

publicity. However, the tour raised large amounts of money, and Marie visited many colleges and even met President Warren Harding.

Many journalists wrote of radium providing 'miracle' cures for cancer. Marie never made such claims, but she did believe that radium could provide a useful treatment. She continued her research into radiotherapy. Her daughter Irène was now developing her own career in science and working at the Radium Institute. In 1926 she married a colleague named Frédéric Joliot.

In 1933 Marie became ill with severe anemia, a blood disorder. Her bones had been damaged over the years by so much radiation. She worked on into 1934, but her life's work was now taking its toll. She was nursed by her daughter Ève. Doctors said she should go to a sanatorium in the French Alps to breathe some pure air. Feverish and weak, Marie travelled on her last journey. She died at the sanatorium of Sancellemoz on 4 July 1934, at age 66.

Two days later, Marie Sklodowska Curie was buried in Sceaux, beside her beloved husband, Pierre, and his family. Her sister Bronia and her brother Józef threw a handful of soil from Poland into the grave.

Below: Marie Curie finally found peace amid the peaks of the French Alps, where she died.

1926
Irène Curie marries Frédéric Joliot.

4 July 1934
Marie Curie dies at Sancellemoz sanatorium in the French Alps.

Marie's Dream

Marie Sklodowska Curie suffered great sadness and hardship in her life. Even so, she never lost sight of her dream. She was driven by a belief in science and progress, in hard work, education and helping others.

As a scientist, Marie Curie was a genius at measuring and working out methods for experiments. Her research into radiation, with her husband, Pierre, helped others discover the structure of the atom, one of the greatest puzzles of the universe. Radiation itself turned out to be extremely dangerous, but it also proved to be very useful in areas such as treating cancer, generating electricity and diagnosing medical problems.

Marie Curie lived in an age when women had few opportunities, but she let nothing stand in her way.

Above: In 1935 Marie's daughter Irène and her husband, Frédéric, received a Nobel Prize in chemistry. They had discovered artificial radioactivity.

'It is important to make a dream of life, and of a dream, reality.'
Pierre Curie

1935
Irène Joliot-Curie and her husband, Frédéric, receive the Nobel Prize in chemistry.

1937
Ève Curie, who became a successful journalist, publishes a biography of her mother.

Not only did she become a scientist, but she also was the winner of two Nobel Prizes. Marie became one of history's best-known scientists. In 1943 a popular film was made of her life. Her story has probably inspired many young people, especially girls, to take up science.

The Panthéon in Paris is an impressive building, a memorial to France's greatest men – and, from 1995, women too. On April 20 of that year, the remains of Pierre and Marie Curie were taken from Sceaux and reburied in the Panthéon. There was a guard of honour, bands and fine speeches from the president of France and the president of Poland.

This was a strangely grand affair to commemorate two shy people who had always tried to avoid publicity in their personal lives. But then these had been no ordinary lives.

Left: A long white carpet stretches to the steps of the Panthéon in Paris. This 1995 ceremony was in honour of Pierre and Marie Curie.

1958
Hélène Langevin-Joliot, Irène's grand-daughter, joins the Institute of Nuclear Physics at the University of Paris.

1995
Marie and Pierre Curie are reburied in the Panthéon, Paris.

Glossary

anemia an illness that affects the blood.

atom the smallest single part of an element that is itself made up of tiny particles. These smaller particles include electrons which orbit around a central nucleus made up of neutrons and protons.

barometer an instrument that measures air pressure and can be used to forecast the weather.

certification written proof of accuracy or quality.

compound a substance made up of two or more elements.

current a movement or flow of electricity.

curriculum (plural, curricula) a course of study offered at a school.

decay the way in which the nucleus of some atoms breaks down, releasing particles as radiation.

element a pure, basic substance, made up only of atoms whose nuclei contain the same number of protons.

estate a large area of managed land that is generally attached to or surrounds a large country house.

exile to send someone away from his or her homeland as a punishment.

experiment a method of testing out an idea in a scientific manner, or finding out an unknown fact.

gamma rays rays that have a shorter wavelength than x-rays and are given out by radioactive substances.

governess a woman employed to teach children in their own home.

gymnasium in Germany or Poland, a state-run secondary school.

hydrogen the lightest known element. It is usually a gas, but combines with oxygen to form water.

isolate to separate a substance into its purest or most basic state.

laboratory a scientific workshop where experiments are carried out.

magnetism the attractive force that pulls certain metals together.

manor house a large country house whose owner has traditional rights over the surrounding district.

mechanics the science that deals with forces and motion.

nationalists people who wish to see their homeland become an independent nation under its own rule.

nervous breakdown a period of mental illness, exhaustion or depression.

nuclear reaction a change in the structure or state of atomic nuclei.

nucleus (plural, nuclei) the central core of an atom, made up of a cluster of particles called neutrons and protons.

ore a mineral from which metals can be extracted.

particle a very tiny part of something. Any particle smaller than an atom, such as an electron, proton or neutron, is called a subatomic particle. Particles may consist of matter or force.

partition the division of a country or region into separately ruled parts.

patent a licence to protect an invention as the work of one person, so that no other person can make a profit by stealing the inventor's ideas.

physics the branch of science that deals with matter and energy in the natural world, but not with chemistry or with forms of life.

pitchblende a black ore that contains uranium, radium and polonium.

polonium one of the unknown elements that Marie Curie discovered and obtained from pitchblende.

positivism a belief in social progress through hard work, science and education.

prism a clear object that breaks up light into its separate colours. Raindrops act as miniature prisms, splitting up sunlight to create a rainbow.

quartz a mineral often found in crystal form. Under slight pressure it produces electricity; it has many uses in modern technology, including watches.

radiation the giving out of rays, especially by a radioactive material.

radioactivity the radiation given out by the breakdown in the structure of an atom's nucleus.

radiotherapy using x-rays, gamma rays or radioactive substances to treat a disease, such as cancer.

radium one of the unknown elements that Marie Curie discovered and obtained from pitchblende. It is highly radioactive.

reform school a school for young offenders.

salt compound formed when the hydrogen of an acid has been replaced by a metal.

sanatorium a health treatment centre where people can recover from an illness.

socialist someone who believes that social justice can be brought about by public ownership of businesses and resources.

spectroscope an instrument that is used to study the light given out by substances.

tuberculosis an infectious disease that usually affects the lungs.

typhus an infectious disease that is passed on by lice and fleas.

universe all of space, including all the stars, planets, matter and energy that it contains.

uranium a radioactive metal element.

wavelength the distance from the top of one wave to the top of the next. The rays of light that we see travel with a wavelike motion. So do many other kinds of rays that we cannot detect with the eye. We measure them according to their wavelength. The shortest wavelengths belong to gamma rays. Then come x-rays, then ultraviolet, light, infrared and, longest of all, radio waves.

x-ray a type of ray with a shorter wavelength than visible light.

Bibliography

Madame Curie: A Biography, Curie, Ève, published by Doubleday, Doran & Co, 1937 (this edition translated by Vincent Sheean, Da Capo Press, 2001)

Marie Curie: A Life, Quinn, Susan, published by Da Capo Press, 1995

Marie Curie and the Science of Radioactivity, Pasachoff, Naomi, published by Oxford University Press, 1996

Obsessive Genius: The Inner World of Marie Curie, Goldsmith, Barbara, published by Weidenfeld & Nicolson, 2005

Sources of quotes:

p.17 The memoirs of Helena Sklodowska, quoted in *Marie Curie: A Life*, Susan Quinn

p.41 *Autobiographical Notes*, Marie Curie, Macmillan, New York, 1923

p.56 *Madame Curie: A Biography*, Ève Curie

p.58 Quoted in *Obsessive Genius: The Inner World of Marie Curie*, Barbara Goldsmith

Some web sites that will help you explore Marie Curie's world:

www.aip.org/history/curie

en.wikipedia.org/wiki/Marie_Curie

www.nobelprize.org/physics/laureates/1903/ marie-curie-bio.html

www.ideafinder.com/history/inventors/ curie.htm

www.france.diplomatie.fr/label_france/english/ sciences/curie/marie.html

Index

Acknowledgments

B = bottom, C = centre, T = top, L = left, R = right.

Front cover Corbis/Underwood & Underwood; **1** Getty Images/Hulton Archive; **2** Corbis/Bettmann; **4TL** The Art Archive/Historical Museum Warsaw; **4BL** Getty Images/Hulton Archive; **4TR** Getty Images/Hulton Archive; **4BR** Getty Images/Hulton Archive; **7TL** The Art Archive/Historical Museum Warsaw; **8** Getty Images/Piotr Malecki; **9** Lord Price Images; **10** Getty Images/Robert Harding; **11** ACJC-Curie and Joliot-Curie Fund, Paris; **12** The Bridgeman Art Library/Private Collection; **13** ACJC-Curie and Joliot-Curie Fund, Paris; **14B** The Bridgeman Art Library/Private Collection; **15T** AKG Images/Sotheby's; **15B** Getty Images/Hulton Archive; **16** The Bridgeman Art Library/Private Collection; **18–19** ACJC-Curie and Joliot-Curie Fund, Paris; **21** Getty Images/Hulton; **22** The Art Archive; **23** The Bridgeman Art Library/ Private Collection; **24** The Bridgeman Art Library/National Museum of Cracow; **25** Lord Price Images; **26** Lord Price Images; **27** ACJC-Curie and Joliot-Curie Fund, Paris; **29** The Bridgeman Art Library/ Christie's Images, London; **30–31** The Bridgeman Art Library/Musée Carnavalet, Paris; **30B** Science Photo Library; **31TL** Getty Images/Hulton Archive; **31BR** Photos12; **32** ACJC-Curie and Joliot-Curie Fund, Paris; **33** Scala Florence; **35** Getty Images/Hulton Archive; **36** Getty Images/Hulton Archive; **37** ACJC-Curie and Joliot-Curie Fund, Paris; **39** Getty Images/Hulton Archive; **40** Photos12/Oronoz; **42** Photos12; **43** Science Photo Library; **44L** The Bridgeman Art Library/Royal Society, London; **44CR** Science Photo Library; **45** Science Photo Library/Arthus Bertrand; **45T** Science Photo Library/Scott Camazine; **45BR** Photos12/ Keystone; **46** ACJC-Curie and Joliot-Curie Fund, Paris; **47** Photos12/Interfoto; **49** Getty Images/Hulton Archive; **50** Science Photo Library; **51** Getty Images/Hulton Archive; **52T** The Advertising Archives; **52B** Corbis/Bettmann; **53TL** Science Photo Library; **53CR** Corbis; **53B** Getty Images/Hulton Archive; **54** Getty Images/Hulton Archive; **55** Lord Price Images; **56** Getty Images/Hulton Archive; **57** Getty Images/ Robert Harding; **58** ACJC-Curie and Joliot-Curie Fund, Paris; **59** Getty Images/AFP.